USING THE
LAWS
OF
ATTRACTION
TO FIND THE
Love of your Life

RON MCDIARMID

New York

Using the Laws of Attraction to Find the Love of Your Life

ISBN 978-1-60037-563-7

MORGAN · JAMES
THE ENTREPRENEURIAL PUBLISHER

Morgan James Publishing, LLC
1225 Franklin Ave., STE 325
Garden City, NY 11530-1693
Toll Free 800-485-4943
www.MorganJamesPublishing.com

In an effort to support local communities, raise awareness and funds, Morgan James Publishing donates one percent of all book sales for the life of each book to Habitat for Humanity. Get involved today, visit **www.HelpHabitatForHumanity.org**.

Why You Need This Book

Imagine if someone came up to you and said, "As of this moment, you can have whatever you want in life. Doesn't matter if you want to find your soul mate, a small fortune, or even your dream job. Whatever it is, it's yours, if you want it."

You probably wouldn't believe them, would you? Or, at best, you'd think they were delusional. Sure, they might *think* you can have whatever you want, but be serious.

Well, you'll be happy to find out you really are holding the key to the rest of your life. You *can* have whatever you want, and through this book you're going to learn how to go about getting it. This information is truly transformational!

Using the Laws of Attraction to Find the Love of Your Life is all about how to find the love of your life. It uses principles from the Law of Attraction, and it also incorporates much of what I've learned in my twenty-plus years in the personal development industry. I wrote it because I used to be right where you are. I used to be single, and I spent the majority of my free time looking for "the one." But to my frustration, I never could seem to find her! Every date I went on was with someone who just didn't quite fit.

It was by complete accident that I discovered the Law of Attraction. Once I paired these ancient techniques with my own knowledge of personal development, I experienced a transformation in my life that's hard to put into words. It was truly amazing just what a difference it made.

It wasn't long before I met the love of my life, Jillian. Once it hit me that these techniques really worked, I wanted badly to share them with the world. Jillian and I were, and still are, so happy together! I wanted other singles to find the same joy I had discovered.

The result of that effort is the book you're reading right now. I sincerely hope these techniques bring you all the joy and happiness that they did to me.

Sincerely,

Ron McDiarmid

Contents

Chapter 1: Sex and the Universe
(What the heck is the Law of Attraction?)

Think about someone you know who is always worried about getting sick. Most of us probably know a person like this; they obsessively wash their hands, take loads of vitamins, and use a Kleenex every time they have to touch a doorknob. Every ache or pain warrants a rush trip to the doctor's office, and they never travel *anywhere* that doesn't have a major hospital within a five-mile radius.

If you're smiling, then you know what we're talking about here. And the strange thing is that no matter how careful this person is, they always seem to have health problems. They come down with a cold, or sprain an ankle, or contract walking pneumonia in the middle of the summer. How, you wonder, does a person who constantly tries to avoid getting sick manage to stay sicker than anyone else you know?

The answer is because they're using the principles of the Law of Attraction to get sick, even though they don't know they're doing it.

In a nutshell, the Law of Attraction simply states that *like attracts like*. Whatever you give your attention to is what will manifest in your life. Whatever you consistently think about and focus on, that's what you're going to get. Nothing just happens in your life; good or bad, it's there because you drew it to you with your thoughts.

People often compare the Law of Attraction to listening to the radio. If your radio is tuned in to 95.5 "Oldies all the Time," you're not going to be able to hear 101.7 "Hard Rock for the Hard Soul." When you're tuned into 95.5's frequency, that's what's coming into your radio. Nothing else.

Now, human beings are both the transmitter tower and the radio. We have the ability to send thoughts out, like a tower, and receive them, just like a radio. Every time we send out a thought, that thought has a certain powerful vibration to it. Think of how you feel when you are having a happy thought: you're light, smiling, and feeling good. Well, that thought is affecting your body and your mood. It's a good vibration, and your body is responding to that.

When you have that happy thought you're sending those good vibrations out into the universe. Because like attracts like, you're going to attract and receive more good things in your life because of those good thoughts. When you think good thoughts, your frequency is tuned to receive good ones, and that's what you get.

The same works for negative thoughts. When you're thinking about negative things, think of how you feel: you might be sad, angry, hopeless, or lethargic. While thinking negative thoughts, your body responds to them. You're sending out negative vibrations into the universe, so you're going to continue to receive situations that make you feel negative. Like attracts like.

The universe doesn't make any distinction between positive and negative. It's not going to say, "Oh, Jack doesn't really want negative things in his life, so I'm going to hold off until he's feeling happier." The universe only responds to the vibrations that you're sending out.

Here's another example for you to chew on: you've probably seen those entrepreneurs on TV who seem to have it all. They've got a thriving, successful business, they've got an amazing house and a beautiful family, and their abundance only seems to be multiplying every day. Every time you see them they're always talking about wealth and prosperity, or new opportunities, or how great life is.

Sure, sure, you're thinking. If I was that rich I'd be talking about money and opportunities all day long, too. Right?

Well, stop and think about this for a moment: a big reason why they're so successful now is because they decided to focus on wealth and prosperity before they ever had it. When they started their businesses they might have been eating ramen noodles and peanut butter every night for dinner, but do you think they were focusing on that? Probably not. They were dreaming of the day that their business would be making them a handsome living. They were envisioning having a beautiful house, a successful career, and a wonderful family to share it all with.

Those millionaire entrepreneurs talked about wealth and they focused on wealth, so wealth is what they got. And now, nothing's different. They focus on wealth and prosperity, and so they get even more.

Think about what would have happened if they *had* focused on their ramen noodles and peanut butter. Imagine if every evening all they did was grumble about how hard starting their business was, what a sacrifice it was turning out to be, and how regretful they were going to feel if it didn't work out. What do you think would have happened then?

Well, you can sure bet that they wouldn't be the successful entrepreneurs they are today. With a negative attitude like that, they would have attracted more and more difficult situations into their life. They would have continued to feel more and more like the hard work wasn't worth it. They would have begun to doubt that they'd ever make it, and eventually they would have given up and gone back to their day jobs.

The Law of Attraction is the most powerful law in the universe, and this is good news for us! Why? Because it means that we all have complete power to create the kind of lives we've always dreamed about. All we have to do is start changing our thoughts.

Stop and look around you right now. Your life, right at this moment, is a direct result of the things that you think about every day.

If you're not living in the house you want, stop for a moment and examine why that is. You might often think, "Gosh, I wish this house wasn't so broken down and small."

You know what the universe says to that? Here you go! You're thinking "small and broken down," and you're going to get more "small and broken down." The universe gives you what you think about.

If you're currently in a job that you love, how did you get there? You probably landed it by thinking positively and envisioning yourself being put into that perfect situation. Sometime, somewhere, you had thoughts about that great job, and you believed you'd get it. And you did.

Everyone in the world is the master of their own fate, they just don't know it. So many people feel that they're just drifting along, out of control, and at the mercy of outside forces that have nothing to do with them.

This is false. All of us have the power to be who we've always dreamed we could be. We all have the power within us to achieve anything that we want. All we have to do is start changing our mindsets from doubt to belief, from fear to excitement, from hate to love. We have to start envisioning what we want and know in our hearts that we will get it. This is the first step.

The Importance of Gratitude

The second most important component to the Law of Attraction is gratitude.

Stop and think about the last time you were truly thankful for all the blessings in your life. When was the last time you stopped thinking about all the things you *don't* have and started saying thank you for all the things that you *do* have? If you want to change your life, you must begin by being grateful for all the wonderful things you've got going for you.

So say thank you! Say thank you for the home you've got, for the friends in your life, for the car you drive. Say thank you for the great parking spot you found at lunch, for the free coffee you got from Starbucks this morning, and for the great outfit you found on sale last weekend.

It's truly amazing just how powerful the feeling of gratitude is. When you start appreciating the great things you've got right now, you're sending out a good vibration that will attract more great things for you to be grateful for.

Try this: every morning before you get out of bed, think of something to be thankful for. Really *feel* how special this thing is, be it a person, a thing, a pet, or a situation. Feel in your heart how grateful you are that this is in your life, and say thank you that it's there.

Starting your day with gratitude is an amazing, simple way to start transforming your life. The more you say thank you, the more you'll draw into your life things to be thankful for.

The Importance of Action

Now, before you head off to start daydreaming your life away, hold on a sec. We need to talk about a very necessary step three, and that's taking action. *This is a step that many other Law of Attraction books leave out.*

Many people think that if they just sit on the couch all day and envision piles of money showing up in their mailbox, then it will just appear. And sure, some unexpected checks might show up. But if you want piles of money, then you've got to take some kind of logical action to get what you want.

The reason is because taking action is movement and vibration itself. When you move forward to meet your goals and you believe with your whole heart that you're going to accomplish them, the universe is going to send you the things you need to make it happen. People who can help you are going to show up unexpectedly in your life. Circumstances are going to fall almost eerily into place, and you'll begin clicking along like a well-oiled machine, moving ever forward to what you've envisioned.

If you want the life of your dreams or the person of your dreams, you can't simply close your eyes and wish upon a star. If it were that easy, we'd all be driving snazzy red Mini Coopers down the Vegas Strip with our gorgeous dates in the front seat.

No, you've got to take action to get what you want. You must prepare yourself on the inside by stating what you want, envisioning the outcome, and then get going on the outside by starting to take the necessary steps to you're your dreams happen.

So if you're reading this book, you're probably looking for someone to share your life with. Perhaps you've gone through the mill and had one bad relationship after another.

Well, starting this moment you're not going to think about all those bad relationships. You're not going to focus on the fact that you haven't met someone, or how hard you've looked for that perfect mate. By doing that, all you're telling the universe is that you want more of those situations. What you think is what you get!

Instead, from now on envision what life is going to be like when you find your partner. Spend time each day picturing things you're going to do together. Visualize going to the park, taking vacations, and laughing over dinner. Know, and truly believe, that this person you're picturing is out there. The more time you spend visualizing them in your life, the faster they're going to be drawn to you.

As far as what you can do to start taking action on this goal, we'll be going into that in much more detail in Chapter 3.

Positive versus Negative

OK, so at this point you might be freaking a little, remembering all those negative thoughts you've had in the past. You might be imagining them hanging over your head like a gigantic hammer, poised to send some unimaginable disaster your way.

Well, here's the good news: positive thoughts are hundreds of times more powerful than negative thoughts. It takes much more negative thinking to bring negative things into your life than it takes positive thinking to bring positive things.

So, the important thing here is not to revisit those negative thoughts you've had in the past. Let them go, and let's move on. If you keep worrying about that negativity, know what you're going to get?

More negativity! See, you're catching on. This isn't rocket science, and you won't be tested at the end. The

Law of Attraction is really quite simple, and we'll say it again: you get what you put your attention on. Your thoughts become things.

Easy enough, right?

Becoming Aware

Now that you've got an understanding of how the Law of Attraction works, it's important that you become more aware of where your thoughts go during the course of the day.

This can be a hard thing to measure, especially when most people have over sixty thousand thoughts every single day. How are you supposed to keep track of which ones are good and which are not?

The good news is that all of us have a built-in gauge that tells us if we're focusing on something good or something bad, and that gauge is our emotions. Our emotions will tell us instantly if we're on the right track or not.

Think of how wonderful you feel when you're thinking good thoughts. It's good to feel good, right? Sure it is! Everyone loves feeling good, because this is our body's perfect state. When we feel good, then we're on course. We're doing something right.

When you have a thought that makes you *feel* good, then it's a good thought. It's something you should be focusing on. Your emotions never lie, especially when you learn to listen to them closely. They will always steer you the right way.

Now, think of how you feel when you don't feel good. Those feelings of anger, sadness, jealousy, or frustration bring you down. When you're thinking a thought that makes your mood plummet, then it's a bad thought and one that you don't want to continue giving your attention to.

We can all track our thoughts by the messages that our emotions are constantly sending out to us. All we have to do is slow down enough to examine how we're feeling.

External Influences

It's also important to realize that there are many external things that influence our thoughts, and thus, how we feel.

Think for a moment about the morning news. Most of the time the news is filled with horrifically negative stories of murder, rape, kidnapping, or theft. With all of this, do you really ever feel better from watching the news?

Probably not. Many people who watch the news feel dragged down and negative about all the bad things that happen in the world. For the rest of the day, they go around feeling negative and talking negatively, and thus they attract even more negative things into their lives.

Why would you want that negative influence on your thoughts? You can help bring more positive things in your life by cutting out the negative. If the news drags you down, then quit watching it. If the music you're listening to makes you feel sad or angry, then turn it off. If the magazine you subscribe to doesn't make you feel great about yourself, then cancel your subscription. You can control your day by not giving your attention to negative things.

Conversely, there are many outside influences that make us feel really positive. You may have found a book that fills you with joy to read. Well, why not spend time doing that instead of watching the news? You may have a friend that's always fun to be around. Why not take him or her out to lunch?

By doing things with and surrounding yourself with people and events that bring you joy, you'll feel more joyful, and thus attract more joyful things into your life.

This is going to start sounding like a broken record, but like attracts like. What you think, you get.

It's as simple as that.

The Ebb and Flow of Life

There's something else we need to point out here before we move on to Chapter 2.

Constantly thinking about positive things doesn't mean that your life is always going to be picture perfect. Life has a natural ebb and flow. People die. Friends move away. Jobs are lost. What you must do, however, is look for the positive in every situation that comes your way, because that is how true growth happens.

If someone you hold dear to you passes away, it's a natural part of life to feel sad about it. They're gone, and you're going to miss their presence in your life. It happens to all of us.

What you can do in situations like this, however, is try to find the good in the situation. Admittedly, sometimes this might be hard to do. But it's important to know that we have a choice to how we respond.

Yes, we can wallow in those feelings of sadness and negativity. Or yes, we can try to find that tiny spark of goodness. There is always one somewhere, if we look hard enough.

So keep that in mind. No one's life is ever perfectly perfect, so don't think that using the Law of Attraction means that nothing bad is ever going to happen in your life again.

But now you know that you have a choice. When you're knocked down, you *can* get back up. You *can* choose to focus on something good in the situation instead of wallowing in the bad. How you respond to these situations is all up to you.

Chapter 2:
Get Off the Couch. Now.

Yes, I'd like a cheeseburger, please,
large fries, and a cosmopolitan.
—Carrie, *Sex and the City*

S o we've got the whole Law of Attraction idea down pat. You now understand why it's important to focus on what you *do* want versus what you *don't* want.

Now we're going to take a little break from that and talk about your health. Don't roll your eyes and start to put the book down in disgust, because this really does have a lot to do with getting out there and finally meeting the person you've always been searching for.

Here's the short answer to why: when you exercise and eat right, you feel really good. And, let's all chant it together: *when you feel good you attract more good things in your life.*

OK, so maybe this still is a little bit about Law of Attraction, but it's also just plain common sense. Here's another reason why fitness and relationships go hand in hand: stop and think for a moment about your perfect match. You probably already have an idea of what you'd like this person to be like, so pull that picture up in your mind. Got it?

Good. Now, chances are probably pretty high that you're not picturing someone who has ensconced themselves on the couch every evening, gorging on M&M's and potato chips. Sure, that's fun to do on a rainy day once in a while, but it's not something you want to do nightly.

No, you're probably picturing someone who you'd like to go out and do things with. Perhaps you want to go hiking, or horseback riding, or take walks on the beach. Perhaps you'd like to head out for an afternoon of kayaking, or even just a lazy day walking downtown window-shopping. The point here is that you're probably picturing someone who is healthy and is ready to go out and have fun.

Now, I'm going to share with you a secret that most people who are looking for their perfect partner don't realize. This secret is really the basis behind this book's entire philosophy.

Here it is: *if you want to attract your perfect partner, you first have to become what you're looking for.*

It only makes sense! If you want to attract a healthy, successful partner, then you have to become healthy and successful. Why? Because whatever you focus on, you attract more of. If you want to attract the man or woman of your dreams, then you have to become someone they will *want* to be with. When you become what you're looking for, you attract that into your life.

This concept is so simple, and yet so powerful!

Think about it: if you're always moaning and groaning about your life and yet you're looking for a partner who is upbeat and happy, you're never going to find them. The reason is because you're only drawing people toward you who like to moan and groan. You'll attract lousy dates to you in hordes, and you know what they'll talk about over dinner? All their other lousy relationships, their meaningless jobs, and their nagging mothers. Wow, sounds like an incredible night, right?

Remember: *like attracts like*.

Even if a happy, upbeat person did stumble upon your path, they would not want to be with someone who is negative. Happy, positive people want to be around other happy, positive people.

This is why we need to spend time talking about health and nutrition here. If you want to attract the person of your dreams, you've first got to start working on yourself. When you exercise and eat right, you feel good, and then you start feeling great. And when you start feeling great, you'll start to attract great things.

Exercise—It's Not Just For Die-Hards Anymore

Anthony: *When's the last time you had sex?*
(Charlotte pauses to think.)
Anthony: *If you had to think about it it's been too long.*
Charlotte: *Well, when's the last time—*
Anthony: *10:30 today at the gym!*
—*Sex and the City*

OK, so you've probably heard about a million times just how beneficial exercise is, and if we all could get some action at the gym like Anthony, there'd probably be a lot more people hitting the treadmills on a daily basis.

First, we should consider that our bodies were *designed* to move and work every day. The human body really is a perfect machine. Each part has a function, and when you really stop and examine how they all work together, it's amazing.

Now, our ancestors did not sit at desks all day, and they didn't lie around in the evening watching TV. They worked incredibly long, hard days to put food on the table. There was always a chore to be done, and as a result they stayed trim and fit. Their bodies were doing what they were designed to do.

These days, the story is much different. Many of us sit at desks all day. We walk from the car, to work, and back to the car, and this basically makes up our exercise for the day. When we get home we eat dinner and then relax in front of the television to "recover" from the stressful day at work.

Well, this is one of the main reasons why there are now more overweight people in the world than underweight people. And while it's a great thing that more and more people are getting the food they need to survive, it's still a sobering statistic. The human race is getting fat, and a lot of it has to do with the fact that we don't exercise our bodies.

If you want to start feeling better, you've got to get moving. Your body is crying out for exercise, although you may not be able to hear it anymore. When you don't exercise you are more prone to sickness, fatigue, stress, mood swings, insomnia, and weight gain.

But when you do exercise? You feel great! Your body is doing what it was made to do, which is move and work. You're happier, you can control your weight, you're better able to deal with stress and mood swings, you sleep better, and your self-confidence increases dramatically. All of these things snowball to bring even more good things into your life. Exercise really does give you back so much more than you put into it.

Need an example?

My parents believe that any head problem could be solved with physical exercise. That's why all of us are really good tennis players.
—Charlotte, *Sex and the City*

So, let's look at a few ways to start working some exercise into your life.

1. Take a class.
   If you're not wild about hitting the gym three times per week, then find some sneaky ways to work exercise into your life. Taking a class is a great way to expand your horizons as well as get moving.

   Try making a list of things you've always wanted to try. What about dancing? Water aerobics? Mountain biking? Fencing? Tai Chi? Yoga? Rock climbing?

   Taking a class means you'll be participating and learning with other people, which always makes it more fun. It also means you're less likely to skip a workout. If you're paying a monthly fee and have a set time you have to be there, you're much more likely to show up and do it. So have fun with it! Find something active you've always wanted to do and dive in.

2. Be a kid again.

   Remember what it was like when you were a kid? Every day you were outside playing or doing something. You were exercising, but of course you weren't thinking about that. You were just having *fun*.

   Well, why can't you do that now? There are tons of things you can do now, as an adult, that are just as much fun as when you were a kid.

   - Twirl a hula hoop.
   - Skip rope.
   - Play kickball. (Yes, there are adult leagues!)
   - Join a softball team.
   - Skip instead of walk to the grocery store.
   - Play Horse with a basketball and hoop.
   - Play Frisbee golf.
   - Jump on a trampoline.
   - Play Marco Polo in the pool.
   - Race the neighborhood kids down the street.
   - Go on an aimless bike ride.

   You get the idea. All those games you used to play as a kid can still be played now, and you'll be amazed at how giddy and happy they'll make you feel!

Most of the time, we take things way too seriously. Doing fun activities will loosen you up, get you active, and also get you laughing. It's exercise, yes, but it's exercise for your mind, your body, and your soul, as well.

3. Be sneaky.

There are literally thousands of ways to "sneak" more exercise into your daily routine, and once you get into it, it can get addicting. The better you start to feel, the more active you're going to want to be, so finding ways to get more exercise will start to be a game.

So how can you get sneaky with your exercise? Well, by avoiding all of our "modern conveniences" for one thing.

- Avoid escalators and elevators like the plague: use the stairs! This goes for those moving sidewalks at airports, as well. Unless you're late, why not walk?

- Sneak workouts into the tiny spare minutes of your day. If you're waiting for something to heat up in the microwave, stand up and down on your tippy toes until the bell goes off. Instead of bending at the waist to pick something up off the floor, do a squat. When you stop at a traffic light, tighten your butt and thigh muscles until the light turns green. When you're standing in line, lift one foot slightly off the ground, making your other leg work harder; switch feet every few minutes.

- You can also get sneaky with your household chores. Scrubbing the floor, vacuuming, raking leaves, and vigorously washing windows all count as exercise because you're working your body. Not only will you get a workout in, but your house will also be cleaner as a result!

- Do small sets of push-ups during the day. Push-ups work seven different muscles, and doing five will burn up to ten calories. So, make a rule that every time you enter the living room, you've got to drop down and do five. Every time your child yells your name or the phone rings, you've got to do five (this one is a surefire way to get a great workout in!). Remember, make it fun!

- Work sit-ups into your day as well. Make it a rule that if you're watching TV, every time a commercial comes on you have to do ten or fifteen crunches. While you're waiting for the coffee to brew in the morning, do a set.

- You can easily work more walking into your day by *making* yourself walk. Park far away from the grocery store. Purposefully leave things downstairs so you have to walk back down and get them. Park a few blocks away from the library.

- When you're on the phone at work, stand up while you're talking. Just standing burns more calories than sitting. If you've got a cordless phone, then why not walk around your office?

- Instead of sending an e-mail to someone in your office, why not just get up and go tell them the message in person?

- Get a pedometer. If you want to get active, then you should aim for at least 8,500 steps per day. If your goal is to lose weight, then you should aim for 12,000 or more. Yeah, it sounds like a lot, but it's not as much as you might think. Wearing a pedometer all day can be a fun, informative way to find out just how much you're walking in the course of your daily routine.

Of course, the list could keep going here, but you get the picture. There are literally thousands of ways you can begin to sneak exercise into your day. All you have to do is get creative! Eventually, all these little things will begin to add up. You'll start feeling better, you'll start looking better, and good things will begin to come into your life because of it.

Don't think that you have to jump into some crazy exercise routine to see benefits. If you can start doing some kind of exercise for half an hour, three times per week, that's an excellent start. And if in between your workouts you can do some sneaky little activities like we've talked about here, even better.

Most of all, remember: exercise can be really, really fun! It doesn't have to be a "grueling routine" like most people think. Find activities that bring you joy and jump in.

Nutrition

OK, so exercise is a pretty important component to feeling great. Now we've got to look at what you're eating, because this plays a major part as well.

Food is what fuels everything in our lives. We can't do anything unless we eat and drink regularly, so it's important that we're putting the very best fuel into our body that we can.

Chew on these statistics for a moment: an average Japanese family spends almost 25 percent of their income on food, and their culture has the lowest obesity rate in the world. An average family in the United States spends a mere 14 percent of its income on food, and our culture has one of the highest obesity rates in the world.

What we eat is just as important as *how much* we eat. If we want to stay fit, control our weight, and feel great, then we need to make sure that our diet takes advantage of the best Mother Nature has to offer. This means buying more high-quality, fresh food instead of schlepping over to McDonald's four nights a week.

One way we can learn how to make better choices is by looking at the habits of people who are already healthy and fit. These people, whether they realize it or not, make choices that help keep them thin. They make choices that benefit their bodies, not just satiate their cravings.

So how do they do it? Well, there's no one "magic" answer, but here are some strategies you can use:

- Start each meal with a healthy, water-based food like salad, fruit, or soup. This will give you a great dose of vitamins or veggies—which you need anyway—and will also fill you up and prevent you from eating more of the "calorie rich" main dish. On average, people who consume a soup or salad before a meal eat 20 percent fewer calories at dinner.

- Practice portion control. Instead of sitting down with the whole box of cookies, take out three and leave the box in the pantry. This way you won't mindlessly eat twelve without realizing what you're doing.

- When you snack, eat those snacks slowly. Scientists have proven that the first bite of anything is always the one that is enjoyed the most. After that, we get used to the flavor, and each bite becomes successively less satisfying. So, eat slowly and savor each bite of that cookie. The more you pay attention the flavor and texture, the more you'll realize that you don't need twelve to be happy. Three will do just fine!

- Don't snack and watch TV at the same time! Studies have proven that if you snack while watching a show, you'll eat 40 percent more calories than if you were just snacking in the kitchen. TV is a distraction, so you're not paying attention to your food's taste or texture or if you feel full or not. So, leave your snacking for anywhere *but* in front of the tube.

• Use small plates. The smaller the plate, the less room you have to fill up with food. Another good tip along these lines is to avoid buffets and restaurants where they're known for their large portion sizes.

• Don't skip breakfast! You've heard that it's the most important meal of the day, and it's the truth. Having a well-rounded, nutritional breakfast makes a great start to your day. You'll be more upbeat and have more energy if you eat early in the morning. As the old adage says, "You should eat breakfast like a king, lunch like a prince, and dinner like a pauper."

• Trick yourself into calorie counting. Some people like to compare calories to money. For example, if you're on a two-thousand-calorie diet, then this means that you have two thousand "dollars" (or whatever your currency is) to spend each day. So at breakfast if you have a muffin, an egg, and a glass of juice, then you just "spent" $450. You now have $1,550 to spend for the rest of the day. This can be a fun way to keep track of what you're eating, and "spending" throughout the day.

• Spend most of your grocery money on the outside perimeter of the store. Now, it may not be this way everywhere in the world, but in most Western grocery stores, all the fresh vegetables, meat, and dairy are located on the outer wall of the store while all the cookies, snacks, canned foods, and other processed foods are located in the aisles in the middle of the store. If you want to start eating healthily, avoid the middle of the store.

- Eat lean protein. Protein like red meat is higher in fat, which increases your risk of cardiovascular disease. Protein from sources like fish, turkey, chicken (without the skin), and even beans and tofu is much better for you. They're low in fat, low in calories, and they make you feel fuller for longer.

As you can see, there are plenty of tricks you can use to start eating healthily. Getting active will play a big part as well. Once you start working your body, your cravings for sugary sweets will probably go down. Your body will *want* things that make it feel good. You'll find yourself bypassing soda for water. You'll skip the cookies and eat an orange instead. And as the days go by, you'll start feeling better and better.

Now, let's move on to how we're going to tie this all together to help you find the partner of your dreams.

Chapter 3: Looking For Love

Charlotte: *So, how are you?*
Carrie: *I'm good, how are you?*
Charlotte: *Great.*
Carrie: *I told Aidan about the affair and*
he broke up with me.
Charlotte: *Trey and I never had sex on our honeymoon.*
Carrie: *You win. (Pause.) So should we get more coffee*
or should we get two guns and kill ourselves?
—*Sex and the City*

In today's world, there are now more singles than there are married couples. The statistics vary by country, but the fact is that being single is becoming more and the majority and less the minority. Why are there so many singles? There are many potential explanations— widowing, divorce, homosexuality, or even just peoples' choice (some people really do like being alone!).

No matter what the reason, being single isn't the end of the world. It's actually a great chance to get your life in order and have a lot of fun in the process. When else can you sleep in as late as you want, drink as much as you want, or buy those stilettos you've been eyeing for months without worrying about getting nagged about it?

All fun aside, when you stop and think about it, there's no better time than *right now* to reevaluate your life and goals. Even though you're single right now, one day you're going to be part of a couple (which means you might have to curtail your shoe buying or bar hopping to a more reasonable level …). Until that happy day comes, however, why not spend some time on yourself?

If you start a relationship with your head on straight, knowing what it is that you want, then you've got a much better chance of staying in that relationship long-term. On top of that, reading this book will even save you thousands of dollars on a shrink by telling you just how to do it. Lucky you!

Acceptance

Later that day I got to thinking about relationships. There are those that open you up to something new and exotic, those that are old and familiar, those that bring up lots of questions, those that bring you somewhere unexpected, those that bring you far from where you started, and those that bring you back. But the most exciting, challenging, and significant relationship of all is the one you have with yourself. And if you find someone to love the you you love, well, that's just fabulous.
—Carrie, *Sex and the City*

There seems to be a recurring theme in life these days. Everywhere you look, you see images and words that constantly urge you to be something else.

"Buy this handbag and you'll look beautiful!"
"Read this book and you'll live better!"
"Take home these shoes and you'll look cooler!"
"Drive this car and you'll attract beautiful women!"

See? We've all seen or heard messages like this before. The average person is exposed to fifteen hundred to three thousand advertising messages every single day. Most of them pretend to inspire, but all they really do is diminish your self-worth. They tell you that you're not good enough and that without their product or service, you'll never be good enough.

It's no wonder so many people are confused and unhappy! We live in a world that constantly tells us that we're not worthy. Yikes.

Now, it goes without saying that yes, we can always improve our lives. We can always be better than we are, and striving for change is part of what makes life so great.

But, we need to start this path from a place of self-acceptance first.

Every single person on this planet is unique. All of us are special and amazing. We've all had different experiences, we all have different talents, and we all have different ways of expressing ourselves. And yes, this includes you.

If you want to start getting your life in order, you've got to first accept the person you are right in this moment. This person is special and unique, and this person deserves to be loved. When you stop struggling against who you are, your body can sigh and say, "OK. Now we're getting somewhere."

Wherever you are in life right now is where you're meant to be. Everything in your life has led you to this moment, so of course that's where you are!

So stand tall. Hold your head up. Accept, without flinching or excuses, the person you are right now. Silence the inner critic who constantly tells you're not smart enough to get that job, pretty enough to ask that man out, strong enough to achieve that dream, or witty enough to start talking with that woman. How will you know until you try?

When you can do this with a true heart, you'll be amazed at just how liberating it is. Instead of being blown around by the whims of others or by the thousands of messages you're bombarded with every day, you can turn your back and walk with strength and purpose.

Think of this: how can you expect someone else to love you if you can't even love yourself? Relationships are wonderful, but they're not the be-all, end-all of life. If you want true happiness, you first must find peace and love within your own heart. Once you do, others will see that strength in you and you'll attract the people into your life that you really want to be around.

Accepting who you are is saying yes to yourself instead of no. *Yes* is powerful, positive, and liberating. *No* is the exact opposite.

So say yes. Accept. Love. There is no one in the world like you, even with all your quirks. So begin this journey by loving who you are in this moment. *Yes* puts you on the road to freedom and adventure. *No* simply cuts everything off.

Now, all this doesn't mean you're not going to change; *it simply means you're starting from a place of positive love and acceptance.* And that makes all the difference in the world.

Focus Inwardly

Do any of you have a completely unremarkable friend or maybe a houseplant I could go to dinner with on Saturday night?
—Miranda, *Sex and the City*

There aren't many times when we have a chance to truly be alone. Many people shy away from solitude like the plague. If they do happen to be somewhere alone, then they put on the radio or television for "background noise." They call a friend or head out to go shopping. They'll search for anything that will keep their attention off the scariest thing of all: their mind.

When was the last time you allowed yourself to focus inwardly and examine what's there? When was the last time you spent time in conversation with that person you might know the least of all: the real you?

Taking time to focus inwardly can result in some surprising discoveries. For example, you might discover that you're more adventurous than you ever would have thought. You might learn that you've had a secret, yearning ambition to start your own business. You might find out that you've been holding a grudge against a friend for years, and that it'd be better to just let that go and move on.

When we take the time to focus inwardly, we can examine the inner recesses of our hearts and souls. When we take the time to be silent, we can listen to what our hearts have been trying to tell us all along, whatever that may be.

When you start taking time to be with yourself you will be surprised at all the things you'll find out. Our hearts are always speaking to us, but due to the noise and hustle and bustle of daily life most of us have stopped listening. If you want to start changing your life, start taking time to focus inwardly. Listen to what your heart has to say, because your heart will always tell you the truth.

Another reason why focusing inwardly is so important is because of the person you're hoping to attract. Do you want someone with confidence? Do you want someone that knows themselves inside and out and isn't going to bring along a lot of baggage that needs dealing with?

Probably. If you want someone with these characteristics, then you must first become what you're looking for, remember?

Try to make time for yourself every day. Meditate. Have a quiet cup of tea. Lie in the backyard and watch the clouds. Go for a walk.

All of these quiet moments allow you to slow down and listen. They allow you to be born, bit by bit. If you're not used to it, it might be a bit intimidating at first. You might panic, wondering, "What am I supposed to be thinking about? What am I supposed to be doing?"

Relax. You're not *supposed* to be thinking about anything. Just let your mind wander where it will! Eventually your heart will tell you what you need to know, and if you're listening, it will change your life one small step at a time.

Stop Projecting

Maybe the past is like an anchor holding us back. Maybe you have to let go of who you were, to become who you will be.
—Carrie, *Sex and the City*

Raise your hand if this sounds familiar: you were in a relationship once that stunk. Big time. And even though that person and that situation are long gone, to this day you're still going into relationships with distrust and suspicion. Every person you're with is a bit suspect: are they going to cheat? Are they going to pack and up leave with no warning? Are they going to start endlessly nagging me? Are we going to end up fighting constantly a few months from now?

Remember what we said earlier about Law of Attraction: *you get what you put your attention on.* If you're having thoughts like these, then you can bet that somehow they're going to manifest. Keep it up and you'll find yourself with a mate who loves to bicker and nag about every little thing. Or you'll end up with a cheater, or someone who leaves the toilet seat up, or does whatever it is that you're trying so hard to avoid.

You must stop projecting your own fears and disappointments onto this person before they've even had a chance to prove you wrong.

Laney *(to Charlotte)*: *Look, I'm sure you get asked this all the time, but what is your problem?*
—*Sex and the City*

These fears and suspicions are negative forces in your life. Let them go. You're living *right now*, remember? If you're still holding on to these thoughts and fears, you're living in the past. You're letting that bad situation influence the life you've got right now.

So, make peace with it in your heart and just let it go.

This can be tricky for some people. If you find yourself still holding on, try some visualization techniques.

For example, if you were in a relationship that ended bitterly and you're still holding on to it, then imagine that person—and all those bad feelings—trapped inside a bright, red balloon. Picture that balloon floating in your mind, buffeted slightly by the breeze. There is a long string attaching that balloon to you, and all those negative feelings and all those arguments are trapped inside that balloon. Now, imagine a gigantic pair of scissors coming up and cutting the string. Watch the balloon float away from you. Feel lighter. It's gone! You just cut all that badness out of your heart. This is just one simple scenario you can use to visually let go of things you don't want anymore.

From now on, give the people in your life their own chances to prove their worthiness to you. Give them trust, love, and respect, and don't let the past influence your behavior right now. The past is over with.

Live Now

Have you ever been on a search for something you wanted badly, and the more you searched, the more frustrated you became because you couldn't find it?

Looking for a great relationship is very much like this. The harder you search, the more elusive it seems to become. You spend all your time looking, and still you can't seem to find it!

Here's a secret: the harder you look, the more it's going to elude you.

Think about this: remember when you were a kid and catching a butterfly was your sole ambition in life? You could chase them across the field all day, and yet you'd never catch them. Finally, tired out, you'd sit in the grass to rest, quietly watching the clouds. And remember what would happen? That butterfly would fly up and rest on your knee for a moment, a handbreadth away.

The point here is that if you focus on *living* right now, everything that you want will come to you. Stop the endless searching. Spend time investing in yourself. Find out what your dreams are. Set goals you'd like to accomplish. Spend time listening to your heart, and learn to like who you are.

When you start becoming the type of person your partner wants to be with, that is when your perfect match will find his or her way to you.

Action Steps: Using the Law of Attraction to Find Love

So, how are we going to tie this all together? Well, we're going to go through some simple steps that will clearly show you how to start using the Law of Attraction to find your perfect partner.

Step 1: Ask for what you want

You need to ask openly for what you're looking for. Picture this person in your head, and all the wonderful things you're going to do together. *Ask* this person to come into your life.

Step 2: Believe that your partner is on the way

Now that you've asked for love, you must believe with your whole heart that it's coming. *When* it's coming doesn't matter; it could be tomorrow, next week, next month, or next year. But it *is* coming. So have some faith. Don't start thinking that your request has disappeared into the nothingness of outer space. It's out there, and all the people and things you need are lining up and on their way.

Step 3: Say thank you, right now

Remember that novel concept we talked about earlier: gratitude? Well, here's your chance to start practicing. Say thank you, right now, for the love that's on its way to you. Feel in your heart how happy you're going to be when it gets here. It's going to be great! You're going to have a blast with this new person, so start appreciating them right now. Say thank you for everything that's about to happen.

And don't just do this once. You can ask once, but practice gratitude every single day for what's about to happen. Really feel the emotion of thankfulness. When you're grateful for the blessings in your life, even for the ones that haven't happened yet, they'll be drawn to you much faster.

Step 4: Take action

Asking for love, believing it's coming, and being grateful for it in advance are three vital steps to finding the partner of your dreams. But you also have to take action.

Does this mean you've got to go out barhopping every night? Does this mean you've got to hit every club until you can't drink another martini?

Although those might be fun, the answer is no. Taking action doesn't mean you have to go on a frantic search. Remember the analogy we used with the butterfly—you must believe that it's going to find you.

However, this doesn't mean that you should stay home in front of the TV every night. Go visit an art museum! Go roller-skating! Sign up for a Spanish class!

Go out and live your life. Spend time with yourself, and do the things you've always wanted to do. You never know *when* the person of your dreams is going to show up, just that they're going to. Until they do, you've got to get out there and start having fun. Remember, when you're the type of person your soul mate *wants* to be with, that's when they'll show up. So get going on some of your dreams.

You can also take action by making room for this future person in your life. For example, if you're working seventy hours per week, you're not living like you would with a partner. Cut down your hours so that when your partner does show up, you've got plenty of time to spend with them.

Or if you're sleeping in a twin bed, then where is your partner going to sleep when they show up? Sleeping in that single bed is telling the universe, "Yep! This is OK for me! Send more of the same!" Instead, update to a queen bed. Tell the universe you're ready to share, and you've got the room.

Take the time to go over your life and make sure that it's ready to receive this new person. When you take that action, you're sending a powerful vibration out into the universe saying, "I'm ready!"

Chapter 4: Your Life, Only Better

Think about it. If you are single, after graduation there isn't one occasion where people celebrate you..... Hallmark doesn't make a "congratulations, you didn't marry the wrong guy" card. And where's the flatware for going on vacation alone?
—Carrie, *Sex and the City*

O K, so now we're at the stage where you need to start identifying what you're really looking for in a relationship.

If you're reading this book, you've probably been through a few relationships already. You might have been with someone like Carrie's Mr. Big; you know, an elusive workaholic who dashes in at just the right moment to save the day, but always keeps you running after him in the hopes that one day he's going to finally commit.

Or you might have been with someone like Carrie herself; someone who has been through the mill and is constantly plagued with doubts that they're doing the right thing. As a result, you couldn't get them to make the leap, and so you walked away.

Whoever you've been with in the past and whatever stories you've got to tell, none of it matters right in this moment. The reason is, we're starting fresh here. We're going to sit down and create lists to help describe who, exactly, we want to be with. These are our "Musts," as in, "She *must* have a job," or, "He *must* be taller than me." These are the traits you don't want to negotiate on, because every time you do, you end up disappointed.

Our goal here is to stop falling into those "some day" relationships. Raise your hand if any of these statements sounds familiar:

"Some day he'll stop working so much, and then he'll have time for me."

"Some day she'll stop flirting with other guys and finally realize that I'm the perfect guy for her."

"Some day he'll quit lying and finally open up and be honest."

"Some day she'll stop nagging me and finally realize that life's about having fun."

Yeah, sounds a bit familiar, right? "Some day" relationships do nothing but suck away your time and energy, all the while keeping you holding on, hoping that one day that person is going to change.

Every girlfriend I've had wants me to change something. Change your job, change your friends, change your attitude…. The only thing I change is girlfriends.
—Random Guy, *Sex and the City*

What you have to realize, however, is that relationships aren't meant to be "people fixers." You can't start seeing someone in the hopes that you'll change them to fit your needs. People only change when they're ready to, not when they're forced to by someone else.

So we've got to start looking for your perfect person—the person who is already "fixed" and ready to be with you.

But how are you going to figure out what it is you *really* want?

Lists. Lots of them. Think of these lists as your roadmap to your perfect relationship. If you don't have a map, it's sure easy to get lost, right?

Right.

Your Six "Musts"

First, we're going to make a list of at least six traits that identify what your perfect match must have in order for you to be happy.

Now, you might already know what these six traits are. If so, go ahead and write them down. If not, we've got to do some digging to find out what is most important to you.

Your "musts" list includes all the deal-breakers. These are things that every person you go out with from now on *must* have in order for you to be in a relationship with them.

Start by looking at what's important to you. For example, do you want someone who is financially secure? If that's a vital trait and you'd consider breaking up with someone who is broke, then "financial security" is a must for you.

Also consider these questions:

- Is physical beauty important?
- Must you have someone who is always positive and energetic?
- Do you want someone who cares about their health and lives an active lifestyle?
- Do you want someone who is looking to get married?
- Is having children some day important to you?
- Do you want someone who shares your religious beliefs?
- Must they be a good listener?
- Do you want someone who owns their own home?
- Is sense of humor important to you?
- Do you want someone who is an effective communicator?
- Do you need someone with a college degree?

The list could go on and on here, but you get the picture. You need to envision the perfect person you'd like to be with. Write out a description of this person, and then pick out the six traits that you absolutely can't live without. Remember, there are no right or wrong answers here. These are personal choices, so pick what your heart tells you to pick and not what you think you *should* be picking.

Your Ten "Extremely Importants"

Now that we've got your list of "musts," we're going to create another list. By the time we're done with this chapter, you're going to *love* making lists. Hopefully.

The list we're going to work on right now is your list of ten "extremely important" characteristics of a potential partner.

Now, these ten things are not deal-breakers like the first six were. These are things that you'd like this person to have, but if they don't, maybe you can make an allowance.

For example, financial security might not have made it on your top-six list, but if it's still pretty important to you, put it here. Let's say you meet someone next week who is not currently "in the money," so to speak, but he's just recently started his own business. He's got a clear plan for financial success and really seems like he's on his way.

If this is OK with you, then you've got "financial security" on the right list. You're willing to let it slide because this guy is driven and you believe he's going to make it. If, however, this is *not* OK with you, then you should probably put "financial security" on your "must" list.

Got it? Good.

Now, using the same kind of questioning we did before, write down your list of ten "extremely important" characteristics that you want your potential matches to have.

Your Six "Absolutely Must Nots"

(After Samantha's reported on the previous night's weird date ...)

Miranda: *Y'see, this is why I don't date—the men out there are freaks.*

Carrie: *Well that's completely unfair.*

Miranda: *I'm sorry, if a man is over thirty and single, there's something wrong with him, it's Darwinian—they're being weeded out from propagating the species.*

Carrie: *OK, what about us?*

Miranda: *We're just choosy. I'm getting more shrimp.*

—Sex and the City

Look at this list as the exact opposite of your "musts" list. This list is going to be filled with the traits that you won't allow under any circumstances.

A good way to start identifying your "must nots" is to look into your past. If you always fall for the "bad boy" types who end up running around on you (and as a result, you get hurt), then you've got to put "no bad boys" on your list. If you always end up falling for the woman who loves to shop (and as a result, she spends all your money and then takes off), then "no shopaholics" needs to go on your list.

This list is just as important as your "musts" list because these are the things that hurt you, and thus these are the things you want to avoid.

These traits might not come as quickly as the others, so be willing to spend some time on this one. It might take a few days to really identify what you most want to avoid.

Your "Dreams" List

Dreams are a really good way to experiment.... It's like buying a dress and keeping the tags on.

—Carrie, *Sex and the City*

OK, for right now, at least, we're going to take a step back from the person you're looking for and focus for a moment on you. Yep, the spotlight is on, and there's no turning back. We're going to do some digging into what you want to do in your own life.

We need to identify what you'd like to get accomplished in the days, weeks, months, and years to come. What have you always had a hankering to do but haven't done? What do you daydream about when you're waiting to fall asleep at night?

Making a list of your own dreams is important for a great life in general, not just in finding your perfect mate. The reason is because if you don't know what you want in life for yourself, then you're never going to find the person you're looking for.

Think about it: you'd probably love to be with someone who actually knows what they want out of life, right? Your other option is someone who is drifting through every day, unsure what they're looking for or where they're going. That doesn't paint a very appealing picture, does it?

No way.

Remember when we said earlier than you need to become what you're looking for? Well, this is your chance. You need to identify what you want out of life so that you can get going. When you start living your life with purpose and passion, you'll attract someone who is doing the very same thing.

So crack open a notebook and start brainstorming. And remember, have fun with this! If you've always wanted to join the circus, put that down! If you want to go zip lining in Alaska, start your own business, or design clothing (or all of those things), then write it down.

You want a list of at least seventy-five things you want to do in this life—fun, adventurous goals that make your heart race with excitement. They don't have to be huge goals (like starting your own garden or painting your living room the color of cayenne pepper). Just start dreaming and write.

These points and questions might help you get going:

- Where would you love to travel to?
- If you won ten million dollars, what would your life be like? What would you do?
- What did you used to dream about doing when you were a kid?
- What kind of family life would you like to have one day?
- Are there any creative pursuits, like writing, painting, sculpting, or dancing, that you've always wanted to do?
- What about your health? Do you want to lose or gain weight? Run a marathon? Quit smoking? Drink the world's biggest martini?
- How about charity? How would you like to give back to your local community? Would you teach someone to read? Volunteer at a soup kitchen? Start your own dog rescue?
- Look at your career. Are you doing work that brings you passion and joy? If not, what would you really love to be doing? Don't focus on money here. Remember the adage, "Do what you love and the money will follow." Stop thinking of

what's possible and what's not possible; it doesn't matter. Just dream!

- Consider your spiritual life. Would you like to travel to India to visit a monastery? Do missionary work in South America? Meet Deepak Chopra? Go on a spiritual retreat?
- What about adventures? Would you like to sail around the world? Find buried treasure? Climb Mount Everest? Hike across Scotland? Visit every winery in Italy?
- Education: would you like to go back to school and get your degree? Learn to play the piano? Finally know how to speak French fluently? What are things you'd love to learn how to do?

You get the picture here. Remember, if something stirs your heart, write it down. Don't spend time thinking, "Oh, I could never do that." How do you know? If you can dream it, you can achieve it!

We're shooting for at least seventy-five dreams here, and if you can make it to one hundred, even better. That may seem like a daunting number, but trust me, it's much easier than it seems. Once you start dreaming, these desires will start coming out of nowhere! You might be surprised at just what you end up writing down.

Once you have your list, get going on one of your dreams. If you want to attract a great person into your life, there's no better way than to start really living your own. Living with passion and following your dreams sends out an incredibly powerful vibration into the universe, and you'll start drawing this perfect person toward you once that happens.

But that's not the only great thing that will come out of doing some of these things. You'll be having fun! Plus, there is an enormous sense of satisfaction when you get to cross something off your list.

Visit Morocco? Done!

Learn how to grow tomatoes? Done!

Win a fencing competition? Done!

It's a feeling that you really have to experience for yourself.

Learning to Connect

Samantha: *Tell me why we're going to this again?*
Carrie: *She's an old friend going through a breakup. We're being supportive.*
Samantha: *On a Friday night?*
Charlotte: *She tried to kill herself!*
Miranda: *It was six Advil!*
Charlotte: *On an empty stomach!*
—*Sex and the City*

Sometimes it can feel hard to connect with other people. You might feel that they don't know where you're coming from or that they could never understand you or what you've been through.

When you really stop and think about it, however, every single person on the planet has the same types of experiences.

Sure, we might not have been in Carrie's shoes in *Sex and the City* when the love of her life, Mr. Big, decided he was leaving New York to move to California. But we've all been heartbroken just like her. We've all experienced that feeling of devastation when we learn something so profound that all the air seems to get sucked out the room while we're left standing there, alone and helpless.

No, we all don't have the exact same experiences. But we do experience the same things. We all experience joy, and laughter, and passion. We've all experienced sadness, anger, frustration, or jealousy. We've all accomplished a dream, no matter how small it is, and we've all had setbacks where something we thought we had within our grasp get snatched away at the last moment. Yes, there were different specific circumstances for each of us, but our experiences are basically the same.

If you keep this in mind, you can realize that connecting with the people around you isn't nearly as difficult as you might think it is.

You think they don't know what you're going through? Well, how do you know? Maybe they didn't get dumped by Ms. So-and-so like you just did, but they've been dumped by someone else. They know how devastating it is, and they can probably up offer some words of advice or at the very least lend an understanding ear.

Every person in the world is connected by these experiences. We're all out here, living our lives and doing the best we can. We're all experiencing happiness, sleeplessness, sadness, and love. *And we're all in this together.*

The point here? Well, it's this: go out into the world with an open heart. Stop thinking that there is competition or that everyone is out to get you. Be willing to talk with other people. Hear what they've got to say, and be willing to share your own experiences with them.

You never know who you're going to meet or what you're going to learn.

Your Authentic Self

How does it happen that four such smart women have nothing to talk about but boyfriends? It's like seventh grade with bank accounts.
—Miranda, *Sex and the City*

We've all been through times when we've tried to be something we're not. Perhaps we were trying to impress a date, or a friend, or even trying to pull the wool over our own eyes for whatever reason.

Perhaps we've gone through longer "moments"—times when we spent weeks or months trying to be something we were not. Maybe we tried to dress in a style that really wasn't a reflection of who we were. Perhaps we bought a car for the image it presented and not because we really wanted it. We might have lived in a house that said one thing, while our hearts said another.

Whatever the reason, we've all been there at one point or another. You may be there now.

We're talking about your authentic self because when you're trying to be something you're not, most of the time it means you're living in fear. You fear who you really are. And why? Because you don't feel worthy. You don't feel cool, or beautiful, or wealthy, or smart, or whatever it is that you feel you're lacking.

Here's the hitch though: if you don't love and celebrate who you are, how can you expect someone else to? *How can they love you if you don't love you?*

The answer: they can't. Until you love yourself and live your authentic life, you're never going to find the person you're looking for.

There's a reason why the phrase, "Just be yourself!" is so overused. It's because when you're relaxed and comfortable with who you are, people want to be around you.

Think about the people you know who are always looking for validation. They constantly seek approval from the people around them; they constantly make sure that they're not "sticking out" or doing anything different.

These people are like mirrors. They're not themselves; they're the mirror image of everyone around them. Where are their true selves? Tucked down deep, too afraid to come out.

Is this you? Is this how you want to be?

Hopefully not! You're an amazing, unique, special person who has their own take on things. You've got style, and ideas, and things to say. If you're too afraid to voice them, then it's time to start taking some baby steps to get out there.

If you think you can't do this, you should probably close this book right now. Drag it to the trash can and drop it in. Why? Because being yourself is so important to living a rewarding life and finding the person of your dreams that if you think you can't do it, nothing else is going to help you.

Yes, it's dramatic, but that's how important it is!

But you're not too afraid to do this. It might be a little scary at first, but you can do it. Promise.

Need some inspiration? OK.

Imagine yourself at a party. You're talking with a group of friends, scoping out the room, when suddenly a new person walks into the room. This person (man or woman, depending on what you're looking for) holds their head high. They walk with confidence, smiling easily at everyone they see. When they talk, they speak from their heart. They don't fear who they are or what they say, because they *know* who they are. As a result, everyone wants to be near this person.

You can see it, right? Sure you can, because you've probably seen this happen in real life. Authentic people have a quiet confidence that can't be faked or duplicated. They have an aura of irresistibility about them, and it's because at heart, they're completely comfortable with who they are.

When you begin to live your own authentic life, people will recognize the change and be drawn to you.

Here are some tips to help get you started:

- *Stop caring what everyone else thinks about you.* Yes, this might be easier said than done at first. When you think about it, however, what good is their opinion doing you? It's just *their* opinion. If your friends don't like how you dress, then maybe it's time to find new friends. If your neighbor thinks your new house color is ugly, so what? *They* don't live there! Do and say things that make *you* happy. Of course, there's a fine line between doing this and being rude; don't forget that being considerate is important, too.

- *Stop worrying so much.* Yep, you read that right. Many of us worry way, way too much about little things. We worry that our friends will notice we gained two pounds or that we accidently put on two different-colored socks this morning. We worry that we dried out the chicken or that we didn't pick out the right birthday card. The advice here? Let it go. You remembered the birthday, you took the time to cook dinner, and you at least remembered that you needed socks. If they bring it up, then laugh about it! Things aren't going to always go as planned, and it's the little detours that make life so fun, anyway.

- *Be honest.* Being open and honest is one of the best ways to start living an authentic life. Even though it may seem sometimes as if honesty is the harder route, it's actually the easiest. When you're honest, your life is happy and peaceful.

- *Learn to laugh at your bumps.* So you tripped over the curb and stumbled. So you knocked over that vase of flowers or got poppy seeds stuck in your teeth. Laugh about it! When you can laugh at life's little bumps instead of being mortified, you'll start having a lot more fun. Plus, you'll get the people around you laughing, too. And that makes it even funnier.

Learning to be yourself and living an authentic life is one of the fastest tracks you can get on for personal happiness. There is no one on Earth just like you. So celebrate that fact! When you start to believe in yourself and learn to love who you are, you're opening up a way for your perfect mate to love you, as well.

Chapter 5: Fun? Anyone?

When you're a teenager, all you want to do is buy beer.
But once you hit thirty all you want to do is to get carded.
—Carrie, *Sex and the City*

You've probably wondered at one point or another when life got so serious. It seemed to sneak up on you, right? Not too long ago you were playing in the streets, a happy, carefree kid with nothing better to do than build forts or hang out at your friend's house. Life was the regular pattern of school, play, and summer vacation.

Now, however, we've got *responsibility*. We have rent or a mortgage to pay. We get bills in the mail. We go to doctor's appointments, run errands, and instead of using our "fun money" on actual *fun* things, we use it to see our therapists twice a week. Blah.

How did this happen? When did we stop having fun to become staid, consenting, chino-wearing adults? When did we bypass the fun park for the chance to buy cashmere at J. Crew?

If you're like most people, it happened gradually. First you got a part-time job while you were still in school. Then you might have gotten a car. Suddenly, oil changes and The Gap became more important than that ski trip with your buddies. And then you went to college, and then came the laptop, the loafers, and weekly trips to the hot new sushi bar ... and so on down the road. The next time you turned around, you had a place full of things, a full-time job, and a credit card that you liked using just a *bit* too much. Oops.

Well, here's the good news. Just because you're grown up doesn't mean you have to stop playing and having fun. In fact, if more people lightened up and laughed a bit more, the world would be a much nicer place to live.

It's also good to be lighthearted because people are just drawn to others who laugh more. When you're easygoing and fun, people like being around you. You make yourself feel at ease, so others feel at ease as well. When you laugh, they laugh, and that's infectious.

Plus, laughter and fun send out a great vibration. *When you're happy, you naturally draw more things into your life to be happy about.* Remember, like attracts like. The more you laugh, the more you'll have to laugh about.

So here's the million-dollar question: how do you learn how to lighten up and start having fun again?

The answer is: one step at a time.

You can start with some of these things:

- *Start watching comedies instead of dramas.* Life is serious enough already. Why watch movies and shows that bring even more seriousness to your attention?

- *Create a "great day" list.* When was the last time you had a super fun, awesome day? Do you remember what you did to make it happen? What made the day so great? Create a list of things that would enable you to have a super fun day. Perhaps it would be going to the beach, eating lunch at an outdoor café, or playing with homeless dogs at the local shelter. Whatever makes up your perfect day, write it down and try to work some of these things into your life more often.

- *Hit your local comedy club.* Well, don't really hit it, but you know what I mean here. Stand-up comedy or improv is a great way to start laughing. Sure, not all comics are funny, but when you find one that is, you might be amazed at just how much they can make you laugh. They can also teach you how to take yourself a bit less seriously. Life is full of funny things if you just look at it the right way.

- *Start having more fun at work.* In a recent survey, it was found that Google employees are some of the happiest in the world. Why? Because the company fosters a relaxed atmosphere and encourages their team to have a blast and play while they're at work.

  You can start having more fun at work by taking a page out of Google's book. Instead of just taking a coffee break, why not invite co-workers to have tea and crumpets, or cupcakes, or hot cocoa?

  Instead of having boring office supplies on your desk, why not invest in some fun, whimsical ones instead? For example, instead of having a plain file folder labeled "Misc" for files, why not have one that says, "TOTAL CRAP"? Instead of a book on how to get organized, why not get one entitled, *How to Get Disorganized*?

Also, think about having a few toys on your desk to lighten things up. Silly Putty, Slinkies, Play-Doh, and Nerf basketball hoops are great options for taking a quick break to lighten up.

If you happen to be in a leadership role (if you're a manager or business owner), then why not scrap all those boring quarterly sales contests and start having contests that really get your team excited? You could have paper airplane contests, trash can basketball, or challenge employees to build something out of paperclips.

- *Spend less time with super-serious people.* We've all had those friends who live in dark apartments and throw dinner parties that are solemn affairs full of conversations about the stock market or spending trends. Snooze. You'd have more fun talking to a cardboard box, right? At least you can draw on the box …

If you have friends like this, then politely decline when they invite you over. Instead, hang out with the friends that love playing games, telling jokes, and live for last minute road trips to nowhere. These people have a lust for life, and that's who you should spend your time with if you want to have more fun. Their enthusiasm and sense of fun will rub off on you.

- *Practice being silly.* "Borrow" your neighbors' lawn ornaments and rearrange them; see how long it takes them to figure out you're the one who is doing it. Create a really entertaining answering machine message. Hang up twinkle lights even when it's not Christmas. Go camping in your backyard. Buy a Slip 'n Slide. Tell elaborate stories to the telephone solicitors that call your house. Go skinny-dipping. Play spin the bottle. At the grocery store, slip a box of condoms into someone else's cart, and watch what happens when they go to check out. You get the picture ... lighten up!

- *Practice random acts of kindness.* This is a really great way to bring more fun and joy into your life. Random acts of kindness are just that: random things you do that, most of the time, no one will ever know about.

  For example, if you park your car and notice that the car in front of you just ran out of time on their meter, why not put some change in for them? If a friend is going through a tough time, why not bring her flowers and a happy book to cheer her up? If the man in front of you at the grocery store doesn't have enough money to buy all his groceries, why not just pay the difference for him?

  Practicing random acts of kindness can make you feel so good, and they'll definitely bring a smile to your face. Some people even set goals to perform fifty or one hundred such small acts. Believe me, the more you do them, the more you'll want to do them, because they make you feel wonderful!

- *Cultivate your sense of adventure.* Ever been rock climbing? Zip lining? Scuba diving? Water skiing?

   Ever skipped rope with kids? Played basketball on a sunny afternoon? Gone dune-buggy riding? Been up in a hot-air balloon? Gone ice climbing?

   Do things that are out of the box. Instead of running errands, why not go for a bike ride? Instead of spending the afternoon cleaning your house, why not go fly a kite? Yes, you've got to do those chores; they're part of life. But so is having fun. *There has to be balance.* Make a goal to do something adventurous at least once per week. Here are a few more ideas:

   1. Learn orienteering.
   2. Go kayaking.
   3. Run around your neighborhood in your underwear or pajamas at midnight.
   4. Play paintball.
   5. Give your next date a piggyback ride.
   6. Buy a unicycle.
   7. Visit the circus and ask where you can learn to be a trapeze artist.
   8. Buy a trampoline.
   9. Buy *The Guinness Book of World Records* and choose a record to break (even if it is eating the most bananas in one minute).
   10. Pick a random restaurant in your town that you haven't been to. Then close your eyes and point to something on the menu. But don't look! Show your selection to the waiter

while your eyes are still closed, and then wait for whatever it is to come to your table.

- *Stop watching the news.* Yes, this has been brought up before, but it bears repeating. Do you ever really feel better from watching the news? Probably not! So cut it out. Instead, watch a cartoon or your local comedy channel. Read a funny book, or look up jokes on the Internet. There are a ton of better things you could be doing than getting dragged down by the doom and gloom of local news.

Creating a Personal Toy Chest

Miranda: *What's in your goodie drawer? Robert's Rules of Order?*
Charlotte: *I don't have a goodie drawer.*
Carrie: *Oh, everybody has a goodie drawer.*
Samantha: *I have a goodie closet!*
—*Sex and the City*

Every kid has a toy chest of some kind. It's a secret stash of delights that are pulled out when fun and entertainment are needed.

Just because you're grown up now doesn't mean you can't have a toy chest. Creating a toy chest that's all your own is a great way to have fun. It can also be a wonderful way to pick yourself up when you've had a rough day. One trip to your toy chest and *voilà*! You pull out something simply fabulous that instantly cheers you up.

Here are a few ideas of things you can put in your toy chest. They are, of course, just ideas. Take what you will and go from there.

- Gourmet chocolate
- Delia Ephron's book, *How to Eat Like a Child: And Other Lessons in Not Being A Grown-up*
- Water guns for the next sunny day with your friends
- New, cozy pajamas
- A leather journal
- A new comedy DVD that you've been dying to watch
- Luxury shower gel
- A "Learn to Juggle" kit
- An Etch A Sketch
- A painting kit
- A yo-yo
- A "Learn to Draw Cartoons" book
- Greeting cards to send to someone
- A jar of bubbles
- A *Calvin and Hobbes* comic book

Cultivating Your Creativity

OK, stop moaning. It's OK if you can't paint like da Vinci, draw like M. C. Escher, or even write as well as John Grisham. You don't have to be fabulous at something to get started.

Cultivating your creativity is a great way to add some more fun to your life. When all you do are the things you *need* to do, your life slowly begins to resemble a brown paper bag; and brown paper bags are no fun unless you're a bottle of vodka or you're on an airplane during a major thunderstorm.

Most people spend little or no time in creative pursuit. They may want to, but they don't think they have the time.

Well, the mission here is to get you off of "autopilot." Life is so much better when you're having fun!

Creative acts are very much like play. They allow you to cut loose and just *do* something. When you stop trying to be perfect, you can allow that fun child within you to shine.

You also might start noticing the world around you. When was the last time you really looked at your best friend, and what a great smile she's got? When was the last time you looked up at the clouds to find a hidden picture in one of them? If the answer is "more than a week," then we've got some work to do.

Try some of these ideas to bring more creativity into your life:

- Watch less TV. They don't call it the "boob tube" for nothing.
- Take a dance class.
- Visit an art museum.
- Keep a journal.
- Take a pottery class.
- Paint your walls bright, stimulating colors. Ditch the neutrals!
- Write a story.
- Volunteer at a children's after-school art program.
- Learn basket weaving.
- Volunteer to help build a float for a parade.
- Learn to knit.
- Make some fake business cards to hand out to people you'll never see again (want to be an international diplomat? An astronaut? A cowboy?).
- Design a new outfit for yourself.

- Write a haiku.
- Learn a new instrument, like the sitar or didgeridoo.
- Learn calligraphy.
- Take an acting class.
- Give yourself a henna tattoo.
- Learn glassblowing.

These suggestions are only the tip of the iceberg. There are literally thousands of ways you can start getting creative in your life.

The Big Date: Ways to Ditch the "Dinner and Drinks" Scenario

(Carrie brought Miranda along for a double non-date ...)
Miranda *(looks at watch)*: *I have to go feed my cat.*
Carrie *(voiceover)*: *Miranda had invoked our code phrase, honed over years of bad parties, awful dates, and phone calls that wouldn't end. Unfortunately, I wasn't ready to accept defeat. (Out loud.) I thought you already fed your cat.*
Miranda: *I have to feed it again.*
Manhattan guy: *Cat people—all freaks.*
—*Sex and the City*

How many dates have you been on by now? Wait—er, don't answer that. To rephrase the question, how many dates have you been on where you went to dinner and then had drinks or watched a movie?

OK, snooze. That routine has been done to death. If you want to stand out in the dating scene, why not try something different with your next date? Dating is the perfect chance for you to have a blast with someone new, but most people don't want to take the chance that their date won't be open to something adventurous. So they play the "boring and safe" routine of dinner and a movie.

Well, if you want to start having more fun in your life, don't neglect your dating life. It's the perfect chance for you to "dare to be different."

Try some of these ideas on your next date:

- If you've got a daytime date and both of you have the afternoon free, why not get in the car and just start driving? You can pack a picnic lunch and see where the random roads take you.
- Go play Bingo.
- Go to a fabulous toy store, and each of you spend money on something that seems really fun.
- Go to your local flea market.
- Visit the nearest observatory and gaze at the stars.
- Take your date to a high school game; buy popcorn and hot dogs, and cheer as loud as you can.
- Go play miniature golf.
- Head over to the natural history museum and look at dinosaurs.
- Watch a movie at a drive-in.
- Go bowling.
- Spend an afternoon at the amusement park riding roller coasters.
- Tour a manufacturing plant (breweries and candy companies are good starters).
- Go to a fortune teller.
- Hit some local garage sales.
- If you know where there is a tree swing that's open to the public, why not go swing?

- If it's summertime, why not head to the lake and go swimming? Take a picnic lunch and portable music.
- Go roller-skating.
- Dress up and go test drive a sports car.
- Hit your local library and read children's books to each other.
- Spend some time at your local video arcade.
- If it's wintertime, why not go for a sleigh ride?
- Rent a sailboat.
- Build a bonfire and make s'mores.
- Go fishing.
- If you live near the beach, write a message in a bottle and send it off.

OK, no, you don't have to bow down to me for all these awesome ideas. If you start doing some of this stuff, your dates will freak. Well, in a good way. You'll stand out and have a blast in the process.

All of the ideas in this chapter have one purpose: to bring more fun and adventure into your life. It can be very easy to get stuck in a rut! When you let loose and learn to laugh more, you'll attract more great things into your life.

Chapter 6: Why Your Date Cares about Your Digs

(And what to do about it ...)

Charlotte: *I've never done a number two*
at a guy's place before.
Samantha: *Honey, you're so uptight you need*
to do a number seven.
—*Sex and the City*

So you're probably thinking, if my date cares about where and how I live, then I don't want to have anything to do with them. Who needs that type of materialism, right?

Well, not so fast. Let's put this into a little bit of perspective.

Here's the scenario: you're on a fabulous first date with someone. You're having a blast, and they invite you over to their apartment for drinks and dessert before calling it a night. You're enthralled, so of course you say yes.

Now, imagine them unlocking the door to a scene from *The Exorcist*. There are clothes strewn everywhere, old food on the table, dingy lighting, and there's so much clutter on the countertops that you'd need a map to find the Formica.

Yikes.

Suddenly your euphoric mood just took a nosedive. This person lives like a slob, and you certainly don't want to hang out here. Who knows what is living under the sofa cushions?

Now, you may or may not have encountered a situation like this before, but it isn't tough to see that you don't have to be "materialistic" to care about how a person lives. For example, if your date wants to leave because you don't have granite countertops and stainless steel appliances, then this is materialistic. But if they want to leave because you've got an entire city of cockroaches living in your apartment and you can't sit on the sofa because it's full of dirty laundry, this is something else entirely. See the difference?

How you keep your home or apartment is a reflection of who you are at your most basic level.

In our scenario, your date might have been a blast to hang out with, but his or her home is saying he or she is a confused, disorganized, chaotic person. They don't care about cleanliness or order. On a deeper level, a messy home can speak volumes about a person's confidence level, their emotional baggage, how they handle stress, and many other things.

Think about your home right now. What does it say about you? What could you do to make it more presentable to your next guest? How could your home put you in a better light?

This is why paying attention to your home or apartment is so important, especially when you're dating. Every time you bring someone into your home, you're giving them a real glimpse of who you are and how you live. Every choice you make in your home, from your couch down to your dinner plates, says something about you. And if your toilet is gunky and your closets are filled to the brim with clutter, this tells your date something about you as well. Whoever you bring over is going to notice this stuff, women especially.

So this is why we're devoting an entire chapter to cleaning and organization as it relates to dating. If you bring your date to a clean, well-organized home, they're going to be impressed. They're going to want to stay and get comfortable, and this is a very good thing.

It's also important to spend time on your living space because when you do, you're using the Law of Attraction to say that you're ready to bring a partner home. This is a very powerful way to bring the next wonderful person into your life! So let's focus on that first, and then we'll go into what you can do to start getting organized.

The Law of Attraction and Feng Shui

If you're new to the realm of organizing and decorating, then you may not have heard about feng shui before. For those of you in the dark, here's a quick definition: feng shui is the ancient Chinese art of creating energy balance in a home or office to attract abundance, health, positive relationships, and many other things. (Sort of sounds like the Law of Attraction, right?)

See, many people believe that energy is everywhere and in everything, and when you stop and think about it, they're probably right. Think about how you feel when you walk into someone's home that is bright, clean, and open. You immediately feel happy or relaxed, and without even realizing it, you take a deep, calming breath. Things are good here, and you want to stay.

Now, think about how you feel when you walk into a place that is dark, dirty, and cluttered. You might naturally draw back and tense up. It's uncomfortable here. You do what you have to do quickly and then leave. This is your body's response to the negative energy in that room.

We're not going to go deeply into feng shui here, but it's important to show you the connection between feng shui and the Law of Attraction. Although they're different philosophies, they touch on many of the same principles.

When you use feng shui as a guide for cleaning and decorating your home, you're focusing on aspects of your life that you want to change. While you actually make the changes, you're supposed to *think positive thoughts* about the issue and visualize how it's going to be resolved. This part is crucial!

For example, everyone knows that the bedroom is pretty much the room that symbolizes love and sexual relationships. What signal do you think you'd be sending the universe if your bedroom was dark and cluttered? If you had artwork in there that was depressing or angry?

If there was a gigantic television plopped right in the middle of the room, or a bed that was way too small to share with someone else?

A room like this would be subconsciously saying that you weren't ready for love. It would be saying that you're closed off and too busy dealing with your own issues to let anyone else into your life.

Now, feng shui would suggest you do these things to fix this problem:

- Repaint the bedroom red. Red is the color of love and lust, and it adds warmth and passion to the room.

- Buy a bigger bed and some new sheets. This shows that you're preparing for your new partner. You want them to be comfortable here.

- Get rid of the negative artwork. Instead, put a painting of two lovers, or of any kind of flower that looks sensual (like poppies).

- Ditch the TV. Having a TV in the bedroom is a major distraction and says that you'd rather tune out than talk or play with your partner.

While you make these changes, you should be thinking about the new person that will come into your life. While you are painting, envision all the wonderful things you will do together. While you are buying and assembling your new bed, think about all the great adventures you're going to have in it with your new partner.

In short, *you should be using the Law of Attraction, the power of your intention, to bring this new person into your life*. Yes, changing the room is going to do some good, but it works best when you use your attention to support the changes.

So as you can see, the Law of Attraction and the ancient art of feng shui use the same principles to achieve the same goals. They're different in many ways, but at heart they're the same. Their basic message is: you get what you focus on. Focus and prepare for love, and it will come to you.

Feng shui has been around for thousands of years. If you'd like to learn more about the art of furniture placement and how it impacts your home's energy (and yours as well), then check out David Daniel Kennedy's book *Feng Shui for Dummies*. It's an amazing book for beginners and will give you an in-depth introduction to the fascinating art of feng shui.

How To Get Organized

Aidan: *Don't take this the wrong way, but this place could use a little work.*
Carrie: *I know, but I can't afford it.*
Aidan: *You've got eight thousand bucks' worth of shoes over there.*
Carrie: *I needed those!*
—*Sex and the City*

Hopefully by now you see just how important it is to pay attention to that place you call home. Whether you learn more about feng shui or stick to the Law of Attraction, it doesn't matter. What *does* matter is that you spend some time getting your place in shape. That's what we're going to focus on right now; basic organizing tips you can use to get started.

If you want to propel your efforts into overdrive, don't forget to use the power of your intention! Every time you clean, repaint, declutter, or decorate, be thinking about the wonderful person who is on their way into your life. You're doing this for them. So, imagine their reaction to your beautiful home. Picture all the good times you two are going to have there. No moment you spend visualizing is ever a moment that is wasted.

Speaking of visualization, let's start with a little exercise. Close your eyes and imagine how you'd like your home to be. Picture it clearly; imagine walking in the door. What do you see?

Do you have different furniture? Are the walls painted a different color? Do you have great art on the walls? Is it comfortable? Full of light? Inviting for guests?

This dream image of yours is what we're going to be striving for. It *is* doable; we'll just be working on it one step at a time.

Whatever it is that you see, take a minute to write it down. You don't have to get specific; we're not going to design school, and you won't have to create a project board with fabric swatches and layouts to scale. Just write down quickly what you'd like to see happen. Easy things, like:

- Add more lighting
- Get rid of magazine piles
- Get a smaller sofa

- Paint the living room bright blue
- Finally hang up that original Picasso I bought last year (don't you wish?)

This little list is going to be your rough guide, your vision of what you're striving for.

Someone once said that two halves make a whole. And when two halves move in together, it makes a whole lot of stuff.
—Carrie, *Sex and the City*

Remember, no one gets organized overnight. It's a journey, and if you rush to get your whole house done at once, you're going to get tired and burned out. It's always better to take it slow! When you start, just focus on one room at a time. Better yet, focus on one section of a room at a time. Depending on your "messiness level" (and your schedule), you might not get an entire room done at once. By focusing on one section of a room, you'll be able to see immediate results for your efforts. This will help you keep motivated!

Now, let's jump into some basic organizing tips you might find useful to get started:

- Eliminate the duplicates in your closet. How many black Banana Republic button-ups do you really need? Having six might be overdoing it, don't you think? Why not keep two and donate, consign, or sell the others? The statistic that we wear 20 percent of our clothes 80 percent of the time really is true. When was the last time you wore most of this stuff?

- If you have clothes in your closet that you haven't touched in over a year, then get rid of them. Chances are you won't notice their absence.

- If you've recently lost weight and are holding on to your old wardrobe "in case you gain it all back," what is this saying? It's saying that you're giving yourself permission to fail in your quest to keep it off. It's giving you a safety net. Stand tall! Getting rid of those clothes is saying to yourself, and to the universe, that you're going to achieve your goal. *Don't undermine your success by holding on to that old image of yourself.* You're a new person.

- Eliminate those pesky piles of paper. We get even more mail these days than we used to. The solution? Search online and sign up to get off corporate mailing lists. This will cut your junk mail by at least 85 percent. Not only will you have less junk to sort through each day, you'll also be saving trees.

- When you do get your mail, try not to walk in the door and set it down "to deal with later." All you're doing is putting off an unpleasant task. Try setting up your shredder and recycle bin right by the door you use the most. This way you can sort and recycle mail right when you walk in the door and help eliminate those awful paper piles.

- If your home or apartment looks like a cyclone went through it, then clearing it all may seem overwhelming. So do baby steps! Make a resolution that every day you'll get rid of one item that you don't use. If it's trash, throw it in the garbage. If it's an item that can be reused, donate it. You can also get rid of items on www.Craigslist.com, www.Freecycle.org, or www.Ebay.com.

- Keep your trash bins from overflowing. In feng shui, full trash bins represent old, cast-off things you don't need anymore. It's negative energy. When your trash bin starts to get full, empty it!

- Fix something that drives you crazy. You know that leaky faucet that drives you bonkers? The creaky door that makes your skin crawl? Take the time to fix those things. You will feel so much better when you do, and your home will be in better shape.

- Practice the "one in, one out" rule of organizing. For example, every time you buy a new pair of shoes, an old pair has to get donated. Every time you buy a new kitchen utensil, an old one has to find a new home. You don't have to stick to swapping like items if you don't want to (for example, if you buy a new blanket, you could get rid of something else, like an old jacket). Working this rule into your life means that you will halt the accumulation of "stuff" that plagues so many people. You will reduce the clutter in your home, and only keep the things that really mean something to you.

- Invest in some sturdy canvas bags to take to the market when you buy groceries. Many people hang on to the plastic bags they bring their groceries home in, and boy do these add up fast. These plastic bags are also terrible for the environment! Reduce your consumption, and your clutter, by reusing your canvas bags.

- Install ceiling fans. Ceiling fans help circulate the air in a room, which in turn stirs the energy and keeps it fresh and moving. They can also save you 10 to 40 percent on your cooling costs. How? Because the breeze they create helps you feel five degrees cooler, so you can raise your thermostat a bit.

- Set up a "launch pad" by the door you use most often. This will be one area where everything you need for your day is going to go. It could be a bench with a coat hook on the wall, a locker, or a closet with shelving. Whatever you decide to use, this is where you're going to put your jacket, your purse or briefcase (or both), your cell phone (where it will charge overnight and be ready to go the next day), your keys, your thermos, and whatever else you need when you walk out the door. When you walk in the door from work or school, this is where you're going to put all that stuff away. Don't drag it all over the house! The goal is to keep all this stuff from spreading, reducing your clutter as well as the time you have to spend looking for all of it the next morning.

- Go through your bedroom and remove all your family pictures. This isn't really an organizing tip, but it comes from a principle in feng shui that says that the bedroom is for intimate relationships.

Having pictures of your friends and family in the bedroom is inviting them into the private corners of a space that should be reserved for you and your partner only. Hang pictures that are special to you or symbolize love and happiness. Leave the rest of your home open for family pictures.

- Invest in a shoe rack. Most closets have a disorganized pile of shoes and valuable wall space that is not being utilized. Having a three-tiered shoe rack will maximize your storage space and take care of that unsightly pile. You'll also be able to get dressed quicker in the morning because you'll be able to find what you're looking for.

- Make sure your nightstands are doing double duty. Many people have tables by their beds that have no storage space; as a result, their nightstands are constantly cluttered with stuff like magazines, alarm clocks, tissues, lip gloss, and who knows what else. If this sounds like you, then you need to get a nightstand with at least one or two drawers and a shelf for things like books and magazines. This will keep the surface area clear, giving your room a much neater appearance.

- Make your bed every day. This takes less than a minute and can do wonders for keeping the room visually organized! This is also a subconscious act: you're preparing your bed for its next use. If you leave it messy, who is going to want to come sleep there? No one but you.

- Take a look at your kitchen. Are there piles of clutter on all the countertops? Are you addicted to Williams-Sonoma and have every kitchen utensil ever invented? Do you shop in bulk as if Armageddon is right around the corner? If this is you, some work needs to be done here. The goal: to see the countertops. One trick you can use is to really decorate your kitchen; painting it a new color and putting some "sweat equity" in can really inspire you to keep it clean.

- If you constantly have a problem keeping your countertops free of clutter, then make a rule that nothing, aside from what you're *currently using*, goes there. This might be a hard one to keep; kitchen countertops can be tricky to keep clear. But you must be strict with yourself! As soon as you're done with something, be it paying bills, cooking dinner, or playing backgammon, those materials get put away. Those countertops must be clear every night. You'll have to be like a drill sergeant with yourself at first, but you can do it.

These are just a few tips and techniques you can use to start getting organized. There are literally thousands of Web sites and books devoted to the art of organization, as well as feng shui.

How you live really has a huge impact on your love life (and your life in general). If you live in a well-ordered, clean, comfortable home, you're showing people that you're balanced, happy, and on top of things.

Your living space doesn't have to be a penthouse on Park Avenue or a palatial mansion on the beach! It just has to be the sanctuary that all homes should be—a place that reflects your tastes, interests, and desires, a place that's comforting and relaxing to be in, a place you can bring your lovers and friends to hang out and have fun. That's the true purpose of home, and the more time you spend creating this for yourself and visualizing the great relationships that are coming your way, the faster those relationships will get to you. It's all in the power of your intention.

Chapter 7:
Keeping the Passion Alive

Miranda: *What's the big deal? In fifty years men are going to be obsolete anyway. Already, you can't talk to them; you don't need them to have sex with anymore as I've pleasantly discovered.*

Samantha: *Uh oh, sounds like somebody just got their first vibrator.*

Miranda: *Not first, ultimate, and I think I'm in love.*

—*Sex and the City*

Think back to the first stages of all the relationships you've been a part of in the past. The first six months were like bliss, right? Every smile, every phone call was a delight to your senses. Every touch sent delicious shivers down your spine, and every breath in your ear was enough to send you over the edge. When your partner looked at you, you felt it from the tip of your head all the way down to your toes. Yum!

Yes, the initial stages of lust and love are enough to drive any of us mad with desire. It's a lovely experience that all of us wish would never end.

But somehow, before you know it, it happens. Instead of making love in the bedroom before lights out, you find yourself reading the newspaper while your partner clips their toenails and watches *Everybody Loves Raymond*. Instead of flowers, your partner shows up with Chinese take-out. Your "big night out" no longer means hitting the swanky Moroccan restaurant for a night of fabulous food and dancing, it means pizza and a movie. With any luck, you might stay out past 10:00.

Yikes! How does this happen? Many couples liken it to a slow settling, like dirt drifting to the bottom of a pond. Sure, things start out new and exciting, but slowly routines set in. All that was once mysterious becomes known.

While this level of familiarity and comfort is welcome and wonderful in its own right, it can also be a bit dangerous. Why? Because it's at this stage that most people stop trying. They stop trying to fall in love, to be fantastic, to impress their partner. They've won the game. Why keep at it?

The reason why it's important to keep working at your relationship is because if you don't, it's easy for those flames of passion to die out completely. Any fire that's untended will always go out, right? Right. So if you want to have a relationship that is full of fun and passion for the long-term, you can't stop working at it.

Although many people don't believe that passion can survive the test of time, it's only because they have given up on that dream themselves. Passion *can* survive. What's more, it can grow and become even stronger than in the beginning stages of the relationship. But, this can only happen if you and your partner work at it.

So how do you do it?

In short, never give up trying to love and impress your partner. Ever.

In the immortal words of *Sex and the City*, "Love is a verb."

The Importance of Gratitude (Again)

Loving, delighting, and surprising your partner doesn't mean you have to wrack your brains every day to come up with outrageous schemes or expensive gifts. It's more about your mindset.

Think about your past relationships for a moment. Didn't there come a time when you stopped realizing just how special your partner was? Was there a time when your partner stopped appreciating how great you were?

Probably. It happens to most people at some point or another.

Now, think about this person who is on their way to you. Think about the attributes you've asked for, whatever they are. This person is truly special. They're perfect for you! Aren't you grateful for them?

What's important is that six months or a year down the road you don't forget this feeling of gratitude. You have to keep looking at them with fresh eyes if you want to keep appreciating them, and you have to keep saying thank you for who they are.

See, most people forget to really appreciate their partners. Instead of spending their time and energy focusing on the good things, they slowly begin to nitpick away at the bad things. Soon, that's all they see.

Here's an example: you've had a long, hard day at work. Your partner knows this and decides to swing by the grocery store on the way home so you don't have to go later.

When they get home, you notice that they forgot to get milk. Instead of saying thank you (followed by a hug and a sweet kiss) for the thoughtful gesture, you start complaining that now you can't have cereal in the morning.

Whoa! Back up here!

Now, all of us reading can see clearly where things went wrong in this situation, but in real life this happens all the time. If you don't pay attention, you can find yourself doing the same thing.

If you want a relationship that is going to stay happy and passionate years down the road, *you must start it on the path of gratitude and never get off.* Yes, we've talked a lot about gratitude in this book, and with good reason. Saying thank you and appreciating what you've got can do more for your personal happiness than anything else.

So appreciate your partner. Focus on what's good about them, because when you do, you'll get more good things from them. When you look for goodness, you see and get goodness.

Compliment Them

Everyone loves to be complimented, but most of us don't hear compliments nearly often enough. Sure, we might *think* how sexy our partner looks, or how nicely their clothes look. We might *think* how eloquent they are, or how intelligent. But we rarely say anything.

Well, why the hell not?

What's so wrong with paying compliments? They feel good going out, and they feel great coming in. There is nothing bad about giving a compliment, except maybe when it's insincere. Compliments show our partners that we're paying attention, that we notice when they do something great. Just thinking it doesn't do anyone any good.

So if you want to have a happy relationship, don't forget to pay your partner a compliment now and then. Try for one a day. It's so simple to do, and it will make both of you so happy!

The Power of Forgiveness

Now, you may be shooting for "the perfect relationship," but let's nip that in the bud right now. There is no such thing. We're human beings. This means we make mistakes, we say dumb things, and as a result we get into fights now and then. It happens to everyone.

If you want to have a long, happy relationship, you must learn how to forgive completely. This doesn't mean accepting an apology and then dragging up the argument a week later when something else comes up to be mad about. It means *really forgiving*. As in, it's gone from your heart forever. There's a clean slate, and you're not going to hold whatever your partner did over his or her head weeks, months, or even years down the road.

True forgiveness really is simple when you embrace it. When you forgive, you're daring to open your heart to the other person.

But forgiveness does not mean defeat, and it does not mean that you condone what the other person did or said. Forgiveness is about letting it out of your heart so you can move on. It's about loving them enough to believe they can do better and daring to imagine that they will.

Forgiveness brings peace. It brings joy.

Holding on causes bitterness and struggle.

There are those who will tell you why it is wise to never forget the pain of the past ... but if you look closely at the anger, sorrow, and bitterness that has hardened their faces, then you will also see why learning to forgive is the better of the two paths.
—Guy Finley

Don't Forget the Little Things

Sometimes we can fall into the trap of thinking that we have to do something big and spectacular to show our love. We have to hire planes to write "I Love You" out of clouds. We buy diamonds and sports cars and take romantic trips to Tuscany. While these things are great ways to show your affection, they're also not realistic to do every day.

This is where the little things come into play—and let me say right now, these little things can often bring more joy and love into your life than a new BMW on your birthday. Really.

For example, say you drink coffee but your partner doesn't, and yet you wake up the next morning to find yesterday's dirty coffee pot cleaned out and ready to brew a new batch, saving you from your dreaded morning chore. This little expression of love from your partner is so simple, and yet so sweet. Or if a special occasion like a birthday or anniversary is approaching, why not make your partner a card instead of buying one?

Yes, these are simple things, but don't underestimate how much these little things can impact your relationship. By taking the time to consistently show that you care and that you're paying attention, you're telling your partner that they come first with you. And that's a pretty amazing feeling.

Save Some of Yourself at the End of the Day

How many times have you come home tired and cranky? And then what do you do? You start taking it out on your partner. You complain that the house isn't clean enough, or that they didn't make what you wanted for dinner, and blah, blah, blah. This routine is repeated every night in millions of relationships around the world.

Want to put a stop to it? Good, because it's lousy. Although you can't do anything about the rest of the world, you can make sure that this doesn't happen in your own relationship. To do that, you've got to save some of yourself for your partner.

Think about this: when we're at work all day, we give everyone our all, full steam ahead, 210 percent. By the time we get home, we're maxed out. We have nothing left to give to the most important person in our lives.

Doesn't sound like a very smart way to do things, right? We've got our priorities all mixed up!

Yes, we need to do a great job when we're at work. But we *also* need to keep some energy aside to give to the person who is waiting for us at home. Don't forget that they need some love and attention from you, too!

Add Some Mystery

When you stop and think about what your very deepest desires are, what comes to mind? Not *who* you desire, but *what*. What do you truly desire in a relationship?

The answer is different for everyone, but there are some themes that most people have in common. Many people want excitement, mystery, adventure. Women want to be cherished; men want to be thought strong and protecting. Are these generalizations? Absolutely. Do they have to apply to you? No way. But, these basic desires go to the core of how many people identify themselves as a man or woman. Too often, however, we get caught up in what we think we *should* be feeling.

For example, in today's world, many women feel they must be strong, "go get 'em" girls. They want it all: strength, beauty, success. Many feel they don't "need" to be "cherished" by a man. They've got their *own* inner strength!

And they're right. Women today are powerhouses of strength and fire, and that's awesome.

But whatever happened to that dream every girl had when she was little, of being cherished? Whatever happened to the mystery and excitement of the knight in shining armor?

For most women, the knight got stepped on by a nine-to-five career and a to-do list a mile long.

And what about men? Whatever happened to that dream of swooping in just in time to save the day? Whatever happened to being the hero, of sweeping the girl off her feet?

The point here is that we often get so caught up in playing a role that we forget just how blissfully simple and sweet those core desires really are.

When you think about it, what's so wrong with a little mystery? Why is so hard to come to grips with the fact that yes, maybe a woman *would* like to be cherished and treated like a princess? Why *wouldn't* men like to play the hero now and again?

If you stop and truly look at those old dreams and desires (and they might be buried pretty deep by now!), you might find that it all boils down to a few basic things. Excitement. Mystery. Fairy Tale.

And really, there's nothing wrong with that! You can be a strong woman and still want to feel like a princess at the same time. You can hold women in the highest regard and still want to rescue one now and again.

So liven things up a bit. Guys, be willing to sweep her off her feet. Girls, let him hold the door for you! Neither sex is going to step backward a hundred years if you indulge in a little old-fashioned mystery. It'll be fun, and you might get a bit addicted to it.

What Happens Under the Covers ...

Charlotte: *You broke up with an ophthalmologist over that?*
Miranda: *Orgasm—major thing in a relationship.*
Charlotte: *Yah, but not the only thing. Orgasms don't send you Valentine's Day cards, and they don't hold your hand in a sad movie.*
Carrie: *Mine do.*
Miranda: *You're seriously advocating faking?*
Charlotte: *No, but if you really like the guy, what's one little moment of ooh-ooh versus spending the whole night in bed alone?*
Miranda: *These are my options?*
Charlotte: *And who's to say that one moment is any more important than when he gets up and pours you a cup of coffee in the morning? Let's go! (Bounds off.)*
Miranda: *I'll take an orgasm over a cup of French-drip Colombian any day.*
Carrie: *See, for me, it's a toss-up.*
—Sex and the City

There's no doubt that sex is a very important part to any relationship. Without compatibility in the bedroom, chances are pretty high that things aren't going to last. There needs to be that spark, that chemistry, for passion and love to flourish.

Having great sex is not only key to a successful, healthy relationship, but it can do wonders for your health, as well. Studies have shown that the more sex a person has, the better they sleep and the better they cope with stress.

Sex and the Law of Attraction

Think about how you feel when you have sex, especially when you're with someone you care deeply about. During the experience, you're probably relaxed and full of joy, right? You're full of love for your partner, and you're content with where you are. These are all very good things.

When you think about those great feelings and pair them with what this book has showed you about the Law of Attraction, you can see just how powerful the sexual experience can be.

Here's the idea in a nutshell: when you're having sex, you're experiencing a myriad of emotions like joy, relaxation, empowerment, and love. In terms of the vibration these emotions send out to the universe, they're pretty much the top of the ladder.

Now think about what might happen if, at the moment of orgasm, you focused on your deepest desire and envisioned it coming to pass. *Pow!* You'd be putting the good vibrations you've already got going on to work for you in a very powerful way. Sex creates all these good feelings, but people rarely harness them to manifest the things they desire.

Does this mean that you should spend every sexual experience doing nothing but envisioning things you want? Well, you could, but then you'd be taking yourself away from the experience of sex and connection with your partner.

What I'm saying here is that you should just be aware of the good vibrations you're creating with your partner, and use them from time to time to further manifest the things you desire. And if you can focus on things that include the person you're with, that's even better!

The Importance of Communication

When you start any new relationship, you know that at first things can be hot and heavy. And why not? Things are new, exciting, and mysterious. Every foray into the bedroom is a new opportunity for discovery.

Eventually, however, you or your partner will probably want to try new activities and techniques to liven things up. This is where healthy communication comes into play.

Without good communication, it's easy for hurt feelings and misunderstandings to occur. When you leave yourself open to honest dialog, you can express your dreams and desires and see what your partner thinks. In turn, you can hear what they'd like to try and act as a sounding board. If you both think the idea sounds fun, then you'll be ready to roll.

Many people in long-term relationships eventually stop communicating when it comes to sex, and this is a surefire way for boredom to set in. Sex is a wonderful, important part to any relationship, and keeping the lines of communication open is the best way to make sure that the experience stays fun and fulfilling for the both of you.

Just because your partner wants to try something new doesn't necessarily mean they're dissatisfied with you or that they're "looking around" for someone else. Most of the time, it simply means that they want to try something new. *With you.* Wow, revolutionary, right?

Sex is all about pleasure: your partner pleasing you, and you pleasing your partner. If you can be creative and be willing to learn new techniques and intimate details (like where your partner's G-Spot is, or which new sex toy you think you'd like to try ...), you can ensure that things stay fun and healthy in your relationship.

So stay open-minded! Be willing to listen to what your partner wants, and don't be afraid to let them know what you're feeling, as well. If you can start your new relationship with this kind of openness, then you'll be much happier in the long run. You'll both be willing to try new things and be adventurous in the bedroom, and you'll have more fun because you can talk about your desires openly.

Some Final Thoughts

I probably don't have to tell *you* just how important passion and sex are to your relationships. After reading all that, you're probably rarin' to go, right?

The important thing is to just keep an open mind. It doesn't matter if you're a man or a woman: if you want to keep the passion alive years down the road, then don't be afraid to experiment and try new things.

Incorporate some props into your sexual repertoire. Keeping things a bit edgy and different is a great way to add excitement.

And remember, if you ever get into a situation where you're uncomfortable, just say so! Your partner will not want to continue if you're not having fun. All you have to do is be honest and voice your concerns; it's never worth doing anything you're not happy with just to please your partner. *Both parties* should be having a blast here, not just one.

Conclusion

As you've learned by now, your life is completely within your grasp. Finding your soul mate is simply a matter of asking for them to come into your life and then believing that they're on their way. Prepare for their arrival by focusing on yourself first: remember, when you *become* the type of person you're looking for (and the type of person your soul mate will want to be with), they'll be drawn into your life that much faster.

The amazing thing about the Law of Attraction is that there are no limits to what you can achieve. Yes, this book focused on finding the love of your life, but you can use the Law of Attraction to draw anything into your life. It takes no more effort to draw ten dollars into your life, or ten million. It's simply a matter of following the steps outlined in the book and then believing it's on its way.

I wish you great joy on your new path to discovery using these amazing techniques. Thanks for starting this journey with me!

Yours Sincerely,

Ron McDiarmid

BUY A SHARE OF THE FUTURE IN YOUR COMMUNITY

These certificates make great holiday, graduation and birthday gifts that can be personalized with the recipient's name. The cost of one S.H.A.R.E. or one square foot is $54.17. The personalized certificate is suitable for framing and will state the number of shares purchased and the amount of each share, as well as the recipient's name. The home that you participate in "building" will last for many years and will continue to grow in value.

Here is a sample SHARE certificate:

HABITAT FOR HUMANITY

THIS CERTIFIES THAT

YOUR NAME HERE

HAS INVESTED IN A HOME FOR A DESERVING FAMILY

1985-2005

TWENTY YEARS OF BUILDING FUTURES IN OUR
COMMUNITY ONE HOME AT A TIME

1200 SQUARE FOOT HOUSE @ $65,000 = $54.17 PER SQUARE FOOT
This certificate represents a tax deductible donation. It has no cash value.

YES, I WOULD LIKE TO HELP!

I support the work that Habitat for Humanity does and I want to be part of the excitement! As a donor, I will receive periodic updates on your construction activities but, more importantly, I know my gift will help a family in our community realize the dream of homeownership. **I would like to SHARE in your efforts against substandard housing in my community!** *(Please print below)*

PLEASE SEND ME _____ SHARES at $54.17 EACH = $ $_____

In Honor Of: _____

Occasion: (Circle One) HOLIDAY   BIRTHDAY   ANNIVERSARY

　　　OTHER: _____

Address of Recipient: _____

Gift From: _____ *Donor Address:* _____

Donor Email: _____

I AM ENCLOSING A CHECK FOR $ $_____ PAYABLE TO HABITAT FOR HUMANITY OR PLEASE CHARGE MY VISA OR MASTERCARD *(CIRCLE ONE)*

Card Number _____ Expiration Date: _____

Name as it appears on Credit Card _____ Charge Amount $ _____

Signature _____

Billing Address _____

Telephone # Day _____ Eve _____

PLEASE NOTE: Your contribution is tax-deductible to the fullest extent allowed by law.
Habitat for Humanity • P.O. Box 1443 • Newport News, VA 23601 • 757-596-5553
www.HelpHabitatforHumanity.org

Printed in the USA
CPSIA information can be obtained
at www.ICGtesting.com
JSHW082222140824
68134JS00015B/679

9 781600 375637